TAKE YOUR BABY AND GO!

A Guide for Traveling with Babies, Toddlers and Young Children

by
Sheri Andrews, Judy Bordeaux, and Vivian Vasquez

Bear Creek Publications

Seattle, Washington

Bear Creek Publications
2507 Minor Avenue East
Seattle, Washington 98102

Second Edition
        First Printing July, 1990

Book Design and illustrations by Juli Cobb-Olson

Cover Design by Leslie Kralicek

Typography and production by The MicroPublish Company

Library of Congress Cataloging-in-Publication Data
Andrews, Sheri, 1949-
        Take your baby and go! : a guide for traveling with
babies, toddlers, and young children / by Sheri Andrews,
Judy Bordeaux, and Vivian Vasquez. -- 2nd ed.
        p.   cm.
        Includes Index.
        ISBN 0-936005-03-3 : $5.95
        1. Travel. 2. Children--Care and Hygiene.
I.Bordeaux, Judy. 1948- .
II. Vasquez, Vivian, 1944- . III. Title.
G151.A53 1990   90-791
910.4'0240431--dc20   CIP

To those parents with traveling in their hearts and a baby in their arms.

We want to thank our families, especially our children-- Annie, Elizabeth, Shelley, Rachel, Robin and Max for sharing us with this project, other authors for their support and encouragement and our publishers for their amiable patience.

TABLE OF CONTENTS

Authors Judy Bordeaux, Sheri Andrews and Vivian Vasquez with their children Annie, Elizabeth and Shelley as pictured in the First Edition of *Take Your Baby and Go!*

The authors today: 10 years, 3 children and thousands of miles later. Robin, Annie and Judy Bordeaux, Max, Rachel, Elizabeth and Sheri Andrews, Shelley and Vivian Vasquez.

INTRODUCTION

When our children were infants, we found we both needed and wanted to travel. Yet, as new parents, we were apprehensive about the challenge traveling might present. Through our friendship and mutual interest, we were able to share our experience and knowledge, as well as provide each other with the encouragement needed for those first trips.

The first edition of this book grew out of our extensive travel with babies in the United States. Our experiences range from desert business trips to ski vacations, from Canadian Hot Springs to Mexican beaches. When the book went to print we each had one toddler.

In the ten years since publication of the first edition of this book, our families have grown and our experiences have broadened. We know first hand about travel in Asia and Europe. Our collective experiences include travel with three children, as a single parent and with a child having special health concerns. This edition not only updates the original book, but adds new material. We have continued to learn. We want to share our information with other traveling parents.

Our thanks go to the parents as well as the health and safety professionals who helped us in our writing.

Sheri, Judy, and Vivian

TRAVEL...NOW?

If you are a parent considering taking a baby traveling either for necessity or pleasure, you need to hear two things--do it and plan ahead.

Traveling by plane, train, boat or car with a baby may seem terrifying, but it is easier to travel with a stationary baby than with a crawler or toddler. In fact, if you examine the advantages associated with traveling with your infant, you will probably be more inclined to take your baby and go.

Adjustment to parenting is dramatic. It's easy to become home bound and easy to believe your baby is isolating you from the rest of the world. The truth is, a baby should change your life, not restrict it. You need to seek out the places and events that are important to you. You need to stay in touch with the people you care about and travel can be a part of this.

If you have quit a job or taken a leave of absence, you may for the first time in years have the time to visit relatives, friends or special locations that were difficult to coordinate with your work schedule.

You may sense that many of your relationships have changed since the birth of your child. Parenting can offer a framework for renewing family and friendship ties. A trip to your parents or in-laws can establish or re-establish that feeling of family. A visit with a sibling or a childless friend can start the warm bond of being official or unofficial aunts and uncles.

Another reason for traveling with a baby is economics. Public transportation costs are minimal for children under two. Financially, this time period may be your last chance to travel extensively for many years. As children grow older, the added cost of transportation, lodging and entertainment may limit traveling.

As a couple, traveling may be a way to break out of the home routine. Together you can share the joys and responsibilities of caring for and getting to know your baby.

Not all of the hints included in this book will work for all parents, and they will not all work at one time. You can probably tell after a first reading if a particular idea will work for you and your child. The message we hope comes through is to plan well and go ahead and take off--you'll have a great time!

PLANNING

Thinking ahead about the kinds of equipment, clothing, developmental changes and problems that might arise makes a huge difference in the success and enjoyment of traveling with your child. Careful planning promotes confidence, allows for more relaxed travel and encourages spontaneity. This chapter will cover planning basic for all travel, be it across the street or to another continent.

The Basic Supply Kit

For all of your excursions, however short, you will need a supply kit. This kit should include basics to keep your child clean, fed and warm. It can be as simple as a pocket in your purse containing extra diapers, a bottle, disposable washcloths and plastic sacks for soiled diapers, or as elaborate as a bag containing changes of clothing and food for both you and your child.

The further away from home you travel, the more elaborate your supply kit should become. Be sure to update your supply kit as your child grows.

Develop a "necessity" list of items you find important in your travels. Keep this list in your suitcase or taped to the inside of a closet door.

Equipment

Keep the possibility of travel in mind when purchasing baby equipment. Items such as strollers, front or backpacks, walkers, port-a-cribs or car seats should be lightweight and sturdy. Your local library, hospital, or pediatrician's office should have resource books or information to help you find equipment brands to meet your needs. Especially recommended is the **Consumer Reports Books Guide to Baby Products.**

It is a good idea to save the original carton for traveling. The carton can be reinforced with tape, labeled with your name and address and checked in as baggage when you fly.

The most essential equipment for travel of any kind is an approved car seat. Prior to purchasing a car seat, refer to your car owner's manual for instructions and restrictions that will influence your purchase. Car seat installation instructions should be saved. Locate instructions so they are easy to find--perhaps in a plastic envelope taped to the seat or in the glove compartment.

Anytime your child is in a car she should be securely buckled. Since car seats are rarely available at car rental agencies, it makes sense to take yours with you when you travel.

The position of your baby's car seat changes with your child's development. This should be in the instructions that come with the car seat. Generally, infants should face the rear until they weigh 20 pounds and are able to sit up alone. Preferably the car seat should be buckled in the middle section of the back seat.

The type of stroller you choose to travel with depends on your child and your needs. Umbrella strollers are light weight and fold easily. If you choose this model, look for one that is sturdy with rotating front wheels and back support for your child.

A heavy deluxe model is a good long term investment. These strollers can traverse rough terrain (gravel or cobblestone streets). They often fold down to provide a bed and may have space for carrying a diaper bag. Don't assume that your child will stop needing the stroller when she learns to walk or turns three. A heavy stroller can carry a child up to four or five years of age. This is ideal for extensive sightseeing or travel to places where walking is the best mode of transportation. A stroller can extend your visit to Disneyland or save you from purchasing one in a foreign country.

When your child is very young, a soft front pack makes for easy travel. You can slip it into the diaper bag and have it available at a moment's notice. When your baby is in the front pack, you can maintain eye contact, feed her a bottle and even nurse (with a bit of practice!). You and your baby will feel secure in large crowds. If you are unable to use a car seat when flying, the front pack provides the safest restraint for take-off and landing, provided **you** are secured by a seat belt.

For the older child or one who likes to see the action, the backpack is the answer. Carrying your child this way frees your hands and arms to deal with luggage or another child. Some backpacks have a hinged extension which provides stability for baby while putting the pack on or taking it off. When set up on the floor, these packs make it easy to spoon-feed your little one.

If traveling by plane, carry your child on board in the backpack, then store it in the overhead bin. If checked with your baggage, it will not be available when you need it most. If your baby doesn't have squatter's rights on your back, you may want to consider a soft-framed backpack for luggage while traveling. It is another way to free your hands so you can push a stroller or handle tickets.

A **walker** may seem like an odd piece of equipment to consider for traveling, but for the baby in the pre-walking stage, it can be liberating for both parent and child. A walker can eliminate all those floor level hazards that babies love to explore, like electrical sockets, pet food and dirt. A walker prevents babies from pulling over unstable items in an effort to stand. Your only safety-check required will be for items at "walker level." If your walker has a tray, it can serve as a "high chair" for eating finger foods. Be sure to buy a model that is sturdy, collapsible and stable. A collapsed walker can easily be checked on the airplane or packed in the trunk of the car.

A port-a-crib is a long lasting and valuable piece of equipment to have. If you buy a sturdy, collapsible model with nylon sides, it will last through many years of use and numerous children. It can be used at home when company comes, at day care and when traveling. It can double as a "playpen" when you need to keep your baby off the floor. When collapsed, a port-a-crib will fit in the trunk of most cars. This piece of equipment would not be your first choice to take by plane, but it is probably the preferred item for hosts to borrow or rent for your visit.

As your baby grows, there are situations when a child's harness is appropriate. Consider: boat decks, traffic, docks, cliffs or dangerous scenic viewpoints. Ignore the strange

looks if your active child is safe. Similarly, a **wrist leash** can save you from losing your toddler or preschooler in a busy airport or crowded store.

Optionals

An inexpensive **plastic tablecloth** is a versatile aid. Use it to protect the floor under a high chair, the mattress under a sleeping child or when changing your little one in a less than ideal area.

A plastic, open weaved rectangular laundry basket is a great help when traveling by car. En route, it can hold all your child's clothes or toys. Since you can see through the sides, it is easy to locate a special shirt or a certain book. At your destination, it can be used in the bath tub. This will prevent slipping and exploration of hot water spouts. Make sure to hold on to the basket to keep it from tipping.

Put the laundry basket on the back porch, or entrance to where you are staying to store outdoor equipment such as snow boots, mittens, sand shovels or pails. Use the basket for a quick pick-up for toys and belongings.

You don't have to be in the tropics to appreciate **mosquito netting**. Buy it by the yard in recreational equipment stores and drape it over a crib or playpen when outdoors where bugs may be a problem. If you take the time to find this netting before leaving home, you will avoid searching for it in an unfamiliar city.

If you have an article of clothing with large pockets, include this in your travel wardrobe. The large pockets can be used to hold toys or pacifiers. Consider pinning hotel or motel keys to the inside corner for easy access.

Sample or small-sized baby or cleaning products are good items to stash for your travels. Babies and their clothes are always in need of washing. Some readily available products such as soaps in public rest rooms or the laundry detergent at Aunt Trudy's may be too harsh for your baby's skin.

To Your Baby's Health (and Safety)

Part of your planning should include a talk with your pediatrician. He may have advice on preparing for emergencies: ear problems while flying, teething, ways to deal with sleep variations and tips on how to obtain good medical help away from home. If you would feel more secure talking to your own doctor in an emergency, be sure to carry his phone number on a card in your wallet.

Illness is less traumatic for a prepared parent. Always carry acetominophcn (Tylenol), a thermometer, Pedialyte, (electrolyte supplement for diarrhea) and your favorite baby reference book. Destinations unaccustomed to babies may have harmful substances to explore. Take syrup of Ipecac, but use only under a doctor's orders. It's also a good idea to find the emergency Poison Control Center number for the area you are visiting and keep it by the phone or on a wallet card for a quick reference.

Your baby doesn't have to be at the beach to get a sunburn. Traveling in a stroller or a backpack exposes a baby's tender skin, even on an overcast, summer's day. There are many sunscreen lotions available. Choose one without PABA, factor 15 or higher and apply it faithfully. At the beach, rent an umbrella or create some shade, but remember that reflected light from sand and water can burn. Sun hats and light colored clothing covering arms and legs will help.

An identification bracelet or tag is ideal while traveling. A young child could become separated from you during an emergency. Important information such as name, address, phone and any special problems such as allergies should be included. If you do not have an I.D. tag, write out this information and place it in your child's shoe or bootie. Be certain to attach identification safely so it cannot be swallowed or cause cutting or choking. (See Appendix for source to order these items.)

Clothing

New surroundings and schedules are hard on a baby. Try not to complicate matters by dressing her in new and unfamiliar

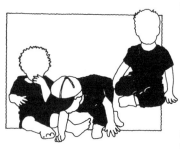

clothing. If you want a comfortable trip, wait until you are at Grandma's to put on that darling new outfit.

If you will be away from home for an extended period, be sure to include some loose fitting clothing for your child. A young baby experiencing considerable growth can outgrow a size of clothing in a month. Take time to think about the range in temperatures and weather conditions you may experience in your travels and pack accordingly.

A hat with a broad brim is great for the baby on the go-- especially one going in a backpack. Such a hat provides protection from sun, wind and rain.

If you use cloth diapers, an adequate supply can be a problem while traveling. They are cumbersome and require frequent trips to the laundromat. Disposable diapers are very convenient, but expensive. If you plan to be in the same location for a week or more, consider arranging for temporary diaper service.

Development

Take advantage of the information available on child development. Be informed of possible changes in your child, such as a bout of shyness or teething which may coincide with your trip.

Expect your baby's eating and sleeping schedule to fluctuate while you are traveling, but try to keep it as consistent as possible. 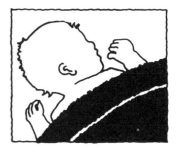 Many infants who normally sleep through the night, quit doing so when away from home. Often they return to their regular pattern after a few days in the same location or upon returning home. Adjusting to a new time zone may take a little longer for your baby than for you. Your little one may be perfectly happy to continue her bed time of 9pm, even though it is midnight at your locale.

Your Needs

In planning to travel with a baby, it is important to address your needs as the primary caretaker. You need to be comfortable and rested to be able to provide for your infant. To accomplish this you must plan ahead. Consider some solutions to possible problems before they arise. Thinking about how to cope with delays, lines or meals will help you in difficult situations. Babies are even less predictable when out of their home environment. Remembering that helps you to keep plans loose and flexible. Be realistic in your expectations of your child and yourself. Conserve your energy when you can by remedying situations that consume it.

Standing in long lines will be tiring for you and your baby. If your child becomes too fussy, ask someone to hold your place while you take a stroll or ask to go to the front of line.

Set priorities for sightseeing and visiting. You may not have the time or energy to do everything you'd like. Driving all over the county to visit friends or relatives can wear you out. Ask people to come see you at the motel or the home where you are staying.

If you are traveling by yourself with your infant, carrying your own food may help. With a sandwich and some fruit, you can eat when it's convenient for you, rather than when the attendant gets to your row or the next restaurant appears on the highway.

Nursing

If you are deciding whether or not to wean your baby before your trip, consider this: while nursing, your baby's food is as available as you are, at the right temperature and needs no refrigeration. If you are thinking about travel to any Third World country (including Mexico), you will not have to be concerned about the water or food for your baby when nursing.

A nursing mother needs to plan her wardrobe with care. You cannot count on a secluded, quiet spot to nurse. Pack clothing that enables you to feed your baby in public. A large scarf or shawl can give inconspicuous cover at dinner time. A small baby blanket in your diaper bag will also serve this purpose while keeping your baby warm.

Rest and fluids are very important to the nursing mother's milk supply. Be sure you get enough of each while traveling. Baby's nap times are wonderful breaks for parents. Your child needs time to sleep. Use the opportunity to remove yourself from sightseeing and parenting and enjoy some sleep or relaxation. Despite your busy schedule, taking time out for yourself will better help you cope with the challenge of traveling with your child.

Coming Home

Make homecoming as easy on yourself as possible. Have a good supply of clean diapers and quick-to-serve food waiting for you. If you can, allow yourself some time to relax before resuming your regular schedule. Coming home a day before returning to work gives you time to get unpacked, do the laundry and catch up on the mail.

PLANNING CHECK LIST

Our Notes:

- *Buy equipment that travels well*
- *Keep a supply bag handy for travel*
- *Consult your pediatrician*
- *Bring health and safety necessities*
  - *Tylenol*   *Doctor's phone number*
  - *thermometer*   *Poison Control Number*
  - *Ipecac*   *ID tag*
- *Think ahead about clothing needs*
- *Diapers: explore options*
- *Prepare for developmental changes*
- *Consider yourself:*
  - *set realistic goals*
  - *conserve energy*
  - *rest*
- *Have home ready for your return*

Your Notes:

DESTINATIONS

Balancing your child's needs with motel accommodations or your host's arrangements is another important aspect of planning. This is where you, the parent, need to be clear about your need for a safe and comfortable environment. As helpful as family, friends and businesses are, they may not be aware of all the potential distractions and hazards their places may pose for your child.

Staying with Relatives or Friends

Staying with relatives or friends is a good way to save money and may mean special moments of late night or early morning conversations. On the other hand, it may create additional tension for you and your child.

Think through all the hazards that may exist. Decks, open stairwells, animals, or swimming pools all may be attractive dangers for your baby. These dangers can be limited by playpens, portable expandable gates, life preservers or having certain pets boarded.

Your host may have chemicals under the sink or valuable vases on the coffee table. Inform your host where your baby is in his development. "My baby is into everything these days" may prompt them to move things up and away, or at least understand when you start doing so. Bring your own safety proofing equipment and use as needed.

Close suitcases at all times. Jewelry and medicine are new attractive adventures for the hands and mouth of your young one.

Your host may also be able to rent or borrow furniture for

23

your stay. It's amazing how many people still have an old crib out in the garage.

Be prepared to be flexible. Your baby may not sleep well in his new surroundings. A trip to an all night grocery store or time spent in the car are good ways to keep your baby from waking the household. Be prepared to entertain your child if he wakes up earlier than the household does.

Your baby will probably be the star attraction of the visit. Eager family and friends will want to hold and fuss over him. It's moments like these when your baby will most likely not

 want to have anything to do with these "strangers". Arriving at a solution to this problem may be difficult for many new parents.

Try holding your baby so he faces the people you are visiting. This gives the "audience" a chance to see your baby's cute face while he is secure in your arms. As an expert on your baby, you may just have to explain that your child is going through the "stranger anxiety" stage. Try turning the attention over to your host. Ask questions, be interested in what they have to say. Basically, get your baby "off stage" and he may warm up on his own.

Hotels/Motels

How you choose to handle your meals will affect your choice in accommodations. If you need to dine in, store formula, or make quick snacks, look for units with kitchen facilities. Hotels or motels that have small refrigerators may suffice if you bring along an electric baby food or bottle warmer. Ask about these accommodations. Things may have changed since the last time your AAA or lodging guide book was updated.

Inquire into the types of restaurants available in the area. This way you can decide whether to eat out or purchase take out food to eat in your room while the baby sleeps.

Secure your room reservations by charging it to your credit card. Most hotels and motels will hold a room until six, but charging will guarantee your room whether you arrive late or early. Being caught in a strange town with a baby and no lodging is an adventure worth missing. If you are renting a beach or ski condominium, ask for one belonging to a family with children. You may get lucky and find one that is child proofed and has baby furniture and toys.

Most motels will rent port-a-cribs by the night. General rental agencies will rent them on a weekly basis for 1/3 to 1/2 the rate charged by hotels.
If none is available and you haven't brought your own, you might want to get a room with an extra double bed. This will allow you to slide into bed to nurse or comfort you baby back to sleep with a minimum of commotion. For safety, push the bed against the wall and ask for extra blankets and pillows for the outer edge.

Consider paying the extra money for a two-room unit if getting your baby to fall asleep is a problem. If this isn't possible, try putting the crib in the bathroom or hanging a blanket over the side of your baby's crib. Sometimes this is just the isolation your little one needs to fall off to sleep.

When you check into your motel or hotel, ask for extra towels. You will need these for your baby. You may need to give a daily reminder to the maid to assure that you get an extra set throughout your stay.

Try and get the ground floor motel rooms whenever possible. This will save you work unloading and loading the car. Taking baby in and out with the stroller is much easier without the stairs.

Always have a pocket light or night light handy by the bed so you won't need to turn on lights when getting up to check your child. This is particularly thoughtful if several people are sharing a room.

Long Term Destinations

If vacation, business, or family circumstances take your family away from home for an extended period of time, your preparations should include a trip to the library. Let your fingers do the walking through the yellow pages or the classified ads of a newspaper from your destination.

Look for apartment hotels or motels. These are specifically designed to cater to the needs of extended-stay travelers. They provide the amenities of a hotel with the space and facilities of an apartment, including complete kitchens and on-site laundry. While some establishments cater to business executives, others are quite hospitable to traveling families. Rental service agencies usually carry a variety of baby furniture to adapt these units to your family situation.

Since you'll be staying in one place for awhile, **consider diaper service.** Most services are on a week-to-week basis. The catch is that diaper service usually delivers and picks up on a scheduled day of the week. If you are washing cloth diapers or your baby's other clothes, disinfect your baby's laundry by hanging it outside in the sun or drying it in the dryer on a **hot** setting.

DESTINATIONS CHECK LIST

Our Notes:

- *Weigh the advantages and disadvantages of various accommodations according to your child's needs; be choosy*
- *Make reservations*
- *If staying with others, plan ahead on ways to cope with your child's particular schedule if it is different than that of the household*
- *Pay attention to safety*
- *Consider diaper service--call ahead to inquire*
- *Consider renting baby furniture*

Your Notes:

RESTAURANTS

Before you became a parent you probably saw plenty of babies out in restaurants. Your reactions to this probably ranged from "what a lovely baby" to, "are those people crazy to bring a baby into a restaurant?" When you dine out with your baby, your experiences will probably range from pleasant to crazed. But once again, planning will help tip your experience favorably.

If you are going to dine out frequently with your baby, invest in a portable travel high chair that hangs on a table. They can be used at home, at the homes of friends or relatives and in restaurants. This high chair puts your baby in the center of the action--this is where she wants to be, and you have more control. Just watch out for exploring hands tipping over glasses, grabbing knives and flinging plates.

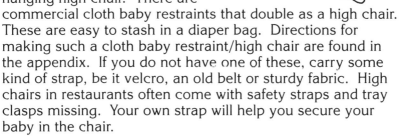

Not all tables will adapt to the hanging high chair. There are commercial cloth baby restraints that double as a high chair. These are easy to stash in a diaper bag. Directions for making such a cloth baby restraint/high chair are found in the appendix. If you do not have one of these, carry some kind of strap, be it velcro, an old belt or sturdy fabric. High chairs in restaurants often come with safety straps and tray clasps missing. Your own strap will help you secure your baby in the chair.

The bib of choice for your baby is big and plastic. Spills will happen. Pack that along with her favorite cup or bottle. Even if your child is old enough to eat something from the restaurant menu, carry something to give her until the food arrives. Portable foods that travel well include cubed or individually wrapped slices of cheese, cold cereal in mini-boxes, crackers, grapes, hard boiled eggs and vacuum-packed food cups that require little or no refrigeration such as pudding, applesauce and yogurt.

Try to have your restaurant meals at a time that is best for your baby. A low-fuss time for your baby is also helpful to your digestion. If these times occur during the less popular time for restaurants, like 4:30 or 9:00, all the better. You will probably feel more secure eating when the restaurant is less crowded and the servers less hassled.

Some restaurants lend themselves better to the baby dining experience. The family restaurant chains are there to serve you. Their menu selections may not be elegant, but they do have working high chairs complete with bibs, crackers,

games and other things to amuse your little one. The entertainment value in these crowded kid-filled eateries is great. If your baby is distracted by the children in the next booth while you enjoy your dinner it will be like getting a babysitter and a meal all rolled into one.

Many authentic Chinese restaurants are informal which makes them a great choice. The variety of dishes allows you to feed your toddler appropriate tidbits from your plate. You can also get a small bowl of white rice delivered to your table to serve her until your food arrives.

If your baby is too fussy to take into a restaurant, consider an old fashioned drive-in. It's easier to tolerate a fussy baby in the car, than a fussy baby and a host of stares in a restaurant.

Weather permitting, packing a take out meal to the park may make for a much needed adventure. Here's a dining experience where everyone can stretch their legs and enjoy the entertainment of squirrels and other park patrons. When you take your baby and go, family restaurants, drive-ins, and picnic parks may seem to disappear from your travel path when it is meal time. To the ever planning, flexible parent this only means challenge, not defeat.

If you have another adult travel partner, have one of you scout out a restaurant before unpacking the baby from the car. Check out the wait line, proximity of the tables and noise level. Basically, will your baby fit into this restaurant or will this establishment offend her--either one shades your experience.

Despite all your planning, your baby may take an instant dislike to the surroundings in the middle of your meal. Depending on weather, locale and time of day, you may want to remove your child from the restaurant while one of you remains to eat, arrange to have the meal packed or both.

RESTAURANTS CHECK LIST

Our Notes:

- *Maintain flexible expectations*
- *Adjust eating times*
- *Choose restaurants carefully*
- *Consider drive-ins and impromptu picnics*
- *Bring your child's bib and utensils*
- *Bring snacks*

Your Notes:

CAR TRAVEL

Car travel will probably be your first adventure with your baby. It may be as simple as cross town for a visit or shopping or as complex as cross country.

Regardless of the trip length, your baby needs to be in a car seat. Unplanned braking or collision may cause you to move forward, but it can hurl an unrestrained baby. Studies show that adults cannot hold onto children weighing over 16 pounds during an anticipated impact of 30 miles per hour.

The position of your baby's car seat changes with his development. He should face the rear until he weighs 20 pounds and is able to sit up alone. The safest position is the middle of the back seat.

If your travel plans include using a rental car, find out if a car seat is available for that model of car. If you need to provide your own car seat, make sure you are renting a car that is compatible with your car seat.

Consider membership in an automobile association, even if your travels will be limited to the area you live in. These organizations provide emergency road service. Car breakdowns become doubly taxing with a small baby along. If your travel is going to be more extensive, an automobile association can provide you with maps, accommodation and sightseeing information for any area in North America.

Ever Ready

Keep a travel kit in your car. This kit might include disposable washcloths, diapers, facial tissues, a bib, spoon, bottle, formula or fruit juice, baby food, some toys, crackers or teething biscuits and other items to carry you through an unexpected delay or change of plans.

When traveling in cold climates a few extra survival items are advisable such as sleeping bags, extra warm clothes, and water. A flat tire or car trouble can go from frustrating to dangerous if your child gets cold.

Traveling in heat requires planning. Carry extra water. A large thermos filled with ice can provide a drink or wet a cloth for a cool wipe. If the sun is beating into the car, move baby's seat or tape a shade over the window. Extended car travel may involve filling up your car with so many "necessary" things that there is no room for the family in the car. Your travel plans may need to include careful wardrobe selection and a trip to a laundromat every couple of days. Consider packing bulky items or clothes in plastic laundry baskets instead of suitcases. The baskets are easy to get in and out of the car. Items in the basket can be seen, reducing the need to rummage.

Do not overlook the value of your cigarette lighter. There are many products that make use of this apparatus. Warm formula or coffee is just a plug away.

A Time to Stretch, A Time to Sleep

A major advantage of car travel is that it allows you to set your own pace and take advantage of baby's pace. Be sure

to include stretch time for him. Even though your baby can not creep, he needs time to kick and wiggle. Take a walk around a gas station or stop for a picnic at the rest stop. Baby is not the only one who will benefit from this stretch break.

Plan your driving around baby's nap time. Many babies find riding in the car soothing and easily lull off to sleep. If Mom and Dad are out of baby's sight in the front seat, it may be the same as shutting the bedroom door for nap time.

If your baby sleeps well in the car, you may want to take advantage of this and drive at night. If you do plan to drive all night, arrange for family members or friends to watch your baby while you sleep. Night driving is especially helpful during hot summer travel when your baby is restless and unable to sleep in the heat of the day.

Unfortunately, on a long trip, your baby won't be able to sleep the entire time. You will need to bring out the entertainment. Some parents find hand puppets to work well. Attach some of baby's favorite toys to the car seat with string or fabric so if your baby throws or drops his toys they are easily retrievable.

But most babies' favorite toys are their parents . A game of peek-a-boo, a song or sitting next to your baby and just talking about the road side attractions or family you are going to visit may be the best entertainment. Baby may not understand your words, but he's got your attention. See the chapter on **TAKE YOUR CHILDREN AND GO** and the appendix for more ideas on entertaining your baby.

CAR TRAVEL CHECK LIST

Our Notes:

- *Car Seat at all times*
- *Bring essentials: a day's worth of supplies*
          cold climate needs
          hot weather needs
- *Stretch time*
- *Think ahead about sleep patterns and schedules*
- *Bring favorite toys*

Your Notes:

AIR TRAVEL

Since the advent of deregulation, much has changed in the air travel industry. Schedules and fares are subject to frequent changes, delays are numerous, flights are more crowded, over booking is commonplace and service is generally not as accommodating as it was before.

In spite of this, travel by air still offers the quickest, most convenient transportation to distant destinations. Courteous personnel can still be found to help if you have problems. The reduced travel time means you will have more time and energy for your baby care and destination activities.

Choosing your flight

Many people prefer to travel during baby's normal sleep or nap period. If your baby is very young and/or can sleep almost anywhere, then this might be a good choice for you. But remember, should baby be unable to sleep, you may end up with an over-tired child fussing the entire flight while others are trying to sleep--definitely not enjoyable! The airlines often offer reduced fares as incentives to fly their late night or "red-eye specials". But beware: these flights have become notorious for overcrowding, over booking and frequent delays.

Flying during baby's normal awake period may provide more predictable behavior. The activities of air travel and the other passengers may be a source of entertainment to your baby. Claiming luggage, arranging ground transportation and adjusting to unforeseen delays will all be easier during daytime hours. Your choice will depend on baby's age, schedule, your destination plans and what is available.

Fly non-stop flights, whenever possible. These flights

eliminate the discomfort of additional take offs and landings on your baby along with the hassles of making connections. Generally this is more relaxing for both you and baby, particularly in winter when many flights may be delayed due to bad weather.

If you must use connecting flights, be sure to schedule enough time to get to your connecting departure gate. Arrivals and departures at large airports can be delayed due to crowded air space and/or weather conditions. The distance between terminals may make connections difficult. If you are connecting on the same airline, sometimes arrangements can be made to hold the connecting flight. Here's where an experienced travel agent can help. Be sure to tell her you'll be traveling with a baby. Ask specifics about connections and distances involved.

Travel proofing your equipment

As mentioned earlier in the book, when purchasing car seats, walkers, strollers, infant carriers or any equipment you may

want to take along on trips, be sure to get cartons that are in good condition. When checked as baggage, the boxes can take a beating, so if you plan to do a lot of traveling, reinforce all box edges and corners with cloth tape before your first air trip. Remember to label the boxes with your name and address, just like you do other luggage. If you do not have a packing box, be sure to label your equipment directly. In the rush to claim luggage, someone could easily pick up a non-labeled car seat or stroller believing it is his.

Seat Assignment

If the flight originates at your point of departure and your ticket permits, the reservationist will usually be able to give you confirmed seat assignments. However if the plane's point of origin is in another city, then you will only be able to "request" your seating preference.

If you're flying at a discounted fare you may or may not have this option. Always ask about seating when making your flight reservations. Choosing a seat that provides the most comfort for you and your baby can make your flight easier and more enjoyable.

In the front section you will find the roomier bulkhead seats make it easier to get in and out of your seat with baby. These seats also provide more storage room for diaper bags and floor area for diaper changes. Many airlines offer infant bassinets that attach to the bulkhead wall providing a safe and comfortable napping place for babies under six months of age. Again, these can be reserved along with a bulkhead seat, but these arrangements need to be taken care of well in advance.

If bulkhead seating is not available, ask for a seat near an emergency exit. Even in crowded planes these seats can offer extra floor space for storage and diaper changes.

Having an empty seat beside you can be a great help especially on long trips. Even if you choose to hold your baby for the entire flight, the extra tray and seat can hold your meal, bottles, and toys. The space can be extra room for stretching or diaper changes. Choosing to fly at less popular times may increase your chances of having an empty seat beside you. Regardless of when you fly, ask the reservationist about this possibility. In most cases they will be happy to hold the adjacent seat empty as long as possible.

Even if you don't get an empty seat next to you, ask the flight attendant to let you know if there are any vacant seats after boarding is completed. The attendant may be able to arrange seat changes for you at this time. If the flight attendants are too busy, be prepared to take this task on yourself.

Removing the seat's inside armrest between adjacent seats will provide you with more elbow room. Ask the flight attendant to show you how this is done.

To assure your prearranged or spontaneous seat requests, you need to arrive at the boarding gate at least 30 minutes before your flight.

Most airlines request passengers with small children to board first so they can settle themselves and their children in quickly. If you are traveling with someone who can help you, boarding the plane at the last minute may mean having less time to sit in a confined noisy area with your baby. A late boarding may, however, limit your ability to obtain an empty seat.

Air Pressure

Babies and young children may have trouble adjusting to the pressure change of taking off and landing because they don't know how to yawn and are unable to chew gum to relieve the build up of pressure in the inner ear.

Encouraging your child to nurse, drink from a bottle or suck on a pacifier or finger when changing altitudes usually helps. For an older child, feeding her orange sections may work well. The tartness of the orange encourages swallowing and the sections make it easier to pace this swallowing over a period of time. Be sure that your child does not have solid food in her mouth when the plane takes off or lands. Sudden jerks could push food back in the throat and cause choking.

It is a good idea to check with your pediatrician before taking your flight. If your child has had a recent cold or a history of ear problems, he may prescribe a decongestant. This medication can be systemic (by mouth) or local (nose drops). If your pediatrician does recommend oral medication be sure to take them in advance of your flight. Nose drops should go in just before taking off and landing. These often have the side affect of inducing drowsiness which could be an added plus on long flights.

Safety

The Federal Aviation Administration (FAA) now requires that all airlines permit approved car seats on flights, provided the extra seat is paid for. All car seats manufactured after January 1, 1981 meet this approval, but there is a catch.

The car seat must have a sticker saying it has met all the applicable safety standards. Without the sticker, the seat will not be allowed for use on the plane.

In the absence of a car seat, a soft carrier that straps securely across your chest may provide the necessary restraint for your baby during takeoffs, landings and the situations where the plane may lurch or hit an air pocket. This will be effective only if you are wearing your seat belt.

The Airline Air Transport Association has recently requested that the FAA require all children under the age of two to be strapped into safety seats during flights, citing the high number of recent infant injuries and deaths. This may mean higher traveling costs. When *Take Your Baby and Go* went to press, this rule had not yet gone into effect.

Currently, airlines differ on allowing car seats without the purchase of an additional seat. Some will let you bring the car seat on as carry on luggage, allowing you to stow it in the overhead bins if there is not an empty seat available. Others will require car seats to be checked in as baggage. Confer with your airline for their specific rules when purchasing your ticket and before going to the airport--things are changing fast.

The Well Dressed Baby

Air travel can also include a variety of air temperatures. These changes can result from flying to a different climate or from simply going to the terminal from the plane. Be prepared to adjust your child's clothing. If your plane is on the runway and there is a delay in take off, this can also cause a change in temperature. If this delay is long and you are uncomfortable, inform the flight attendant. She can arrange for ground support or for the plane to use its engines to keep ventilation and temperature systems normal.

Flying is a good time to take advantage of the new super absorbent diaper products that are on the market. A product that is good for all night may last through the entire flight. If you need to change diapers during your flight and you haven't been seated in a place that you can do this well, ask the attendant for assistance in locating such a place.

Flying with a Toddler

Flying with toddlers is a challenge. They are active, want to do things their way, and can always manage to throw a tantrum if thwarted.

You will need to provide your child with things that are familiar to keep her calm and have things that are different to keep her entertained. You will also need to supply your child with food.

If your child has a favorite stuffed animal or blanket, bring it along. Your child probably relates to this special thing as a source of comfort when she must face nap time alone. This is your child's own stress reducer.

You will need to supply your toddler or any small child with entertainment for the flight. The chapter on **TAKE YOUR CHILDREN AND GO** contains assorted entertainment ideas.

When you make your airline reservations, you can order a special food tray for your child. Special trays have an added advantage of often being served first, but delays and turbulence can slow food service. Have a special supply of foods for the trip that are readily accessible. It is best to have snacks that are sugar free and caffeine free. Carry extra food to account for delays.

Children under the age of four should not eat nuts. This food is hard to chew and small children can easily choke. Nuts are often served with drinks on the plane. Be prepared with a substitute such as cereal or crackers and watch out for well meaning passengers trying to give nuts to your child.

Be aware that sometimes your child will not cooperate and things just **will** go wrong. Don't dwell on it and get on with the rest of your vacation. It won't be the first or last time that a child has cried or thrown a tantrum on the airplane. The next time may go smoother.

AIR TRAVEL CHECK LIST

Our Notes:

- *Choose flight time carefully*
- *Fly nonstop*
- *Ask for seat assignment when making reservations*
- *Try to have an extra empty seat*
- *Help baby adjust to air pressure changes*
- *Carry extra food, clothes, and toys*

Your Notes:

TRAIN TRAVEL

Train travel is an often overlooked option when traveling with young children. The degree of success of rail adventure depends on the quality of service. With a little research and planning, train travel can allow you to be attentive to your baby or share the varied window views with your toddler. Traveling by train removes you from the driving duties of car travel or the confines of air travel.

Your research should include particulars about a train's level of comfort, cleanliness, on-time schedule and safety record. You will want to avoid commuter runs. If you must change trains, don't assume your research will apply to both trains. Make sure your investigation is complete.

A travel agent or reservationist is your starting point This person's services should be sought early in your planning--especially if you are traveling to a popular area.

If several of you are traveling together you may want to look into reserving space in the family seating car. The seats face each other. The floor space in between is good for moving about or diapering a baby.

If your trip involves overnight travel you should consider the convenience and privacy that a sleeper offers. The seats in day cars recline into horizontal positions and the cars are darkened at night, but only you know your child's ability to sleep under these circumstances.

If you have an umbrella stroller, this can go on the train with you. If you have an empty seat next to you, park the stroller sideways for use during mealtime or play time.

Eating in the dining room may not work for you, so bring

food for both you and your baby. You may be able to supplement with something from the snack bar. As with all forms of public transportation, delays can occur, so carry extra food.

Carry your own toilet paper, soap, and towels, since not all trains are equally well stocked for the entire run. Trains also have variations in air temperature so be prepared with blankets and adaptable clothing.

If you are handling both baby and carry-on luggage alone, ask the conductor to call ahead to the station and arrange for a porter to meet you at the platform.

In a world of jet commuters and freeway living, the train may seem unreasonably slow and out dated. But this is an opportunity to sit back, relax and enjoy your baby. You will arrive soon enough, your baby will be soothed by the lullaby of the rails, and you will be ready to meet the challenges of your trip.

TRAIN TRAVEL CHECK LIST

Our Notes:

- *Check conditions*
- *Make reservations in advance*
- *Consider family seating*
- *Carry your own essentials: toilet paper*
                    soap
                    towels
                    blanket or coat

Your Notes:

TAKE A BREAK

Vacations often put parents and children into that unusual living arrangement of being together 24 hours a day. This can be stressful if children are usually in day-care or school with other children and parenting is limited to five or six hours a day. Adults need a break from parenting and kids often enjoy a change from Mom and Dad, especially if it includes other kids! Getting some time off can be tricky and does take planning.

An economical way to take a break is to travel with another family. Friends who have the same interests and children of similar ages make great companions. Rent a house or a couple of condos with enough room to accommodate everyone. Having a kitchen enables everyone to take turns cooking and planning meals saves money. If you have two units, sharing just the main meal of the day gives each family time on their own. Sharing child care responsibilities gives all the adults a chance for some time off, and children have playmates. If you are without a car, rent one for each family. This allows for greater flexibility for sightseeing and scheduling.

Taking a sitter with you may be a solution, if accommodations are roomy or privacy is not high on your priority list. For example, if Hawaii and snorkeling are your idea of heaven, but leaving your baby or young children for a week is just too much--taking a sitter can free you to pursue those underwater gardens for several hours each day and still spend time with your kids. Your children will be cared for by someone familiar and you have a sitter you know and trust. Taking your reliable sitter will require you to pay air fare, accommodations and meals. The cost may be comparable to hiring someone to come to your home to watch your children while you are gone.

Arrangements should be made ahead of time as to your sitter's work time and free time. You may want to write up a contract ahead of time so both you and your sitter are clear about responsibilities and time off. Your contract may read something like this:

BABYSITTING CONTRACT

This is an agreement between Mary Jones and the Smith's for a trip to Hawaii from June 4th to June 18th, 1992.

The Smith's will pay Mary's air fare, lodging, meals and $20 a day. Mary will care for Susie Smith during the flights and trip. She will feed and dress Susie and fix breakfast for the family.

Mary will have every afternoon from 2-5 off. She will have Tuesday and Sunday night off from 6:30 pm until 8:00 am the next morning. If this is not possible, Mary will be reimbursed at the rate of $3.00 an hour for the afternoons and $3.00 for the evenings from 6:30 to midnight.

If your sitter is a teenager, you will be responsible for her welfare. You may want to take a weekend trial trip with your sitter before you take your vacation getting to know how your child interacts with both of you. This will help you clarify additional rules that you may want to put in your contract.

Your sitter should know what vacation activities you plan to include her in. Will she be able to sightsee, beachcomb or snorkel, or be required to baby-sit while you do these things?

Babysitting services are available in most resort and metropolitan areas. These services are usually more expensive than you would pay at home and often require a minimum number of hours. When checking out an agency,you may want to ask the following questions:

> What are the qualifications of the sitter?
> Do they have C.P.R. or health and safety training?
> What experience does your specific sitter have?

Recommendations from friends who have visited the area and have used these services should help ease your concerns. Behave as you do at home when using a new sitter. Leave emergency numbers, go over the rules and spend some time letting your child get to know the sitter before you leave.

If you are traveling to a resort area and must rely on day-care, plan carefully before you leave home. It is worth the extra time and money to make several inquiries by phone. Resorts that advertise day-care can be vague about their facilities. That wonderful ski trip can be less wonderful if the day-care you've planned to use is twenty miles down the mountain. Be very specific when making inquiries and reservations. If the person is not well informed, ask to speak to someone who is or someone who has children of their own. Some areas have terrific day-care facilities on site, but require making arrangements or reservations ahead of time.

Any time someone is caring for your child, limits and expectations should be discussed. Check your surroundings for possible hazards. If your toddler is fascinated by electrical outlets, bring safety covers with you and alert the sitter to this danger. If your two-year-old can open the front door and escape, ask the sitter to dead bolt the lock when you leave. If you do not want a sitter to take a chance with your three-year-old near traffic, be explicit about where they may or may not walk.

Take a good look at the place where your child will be staying, be it a day-care center, a relative's home or your hotel room. Then anticipate the problems that may arise. You know your child better than anyone else. It is better to over explain your limits and expectations than have your child in danger. Your sitter's response to your limits and expectations be it inattention, additional suggestions or active listening will give you a better idea as to whether or not to proceed with your plans or stay with your child.

If you are visiting family, child care should not be as big a problem. Ask a relative to sit or to arrange for someone they know to sit. Again, follow the same rules as with any new sitter. If you are a single parent or traveling alone with your baby or other children, you may need to be assertive in asking for assistance, even with relatives. Your spouse and you probably have worked out relief time for each other and can anticipate when each other needs help with your children. Friends and family may not be as intuitive.

If you have planned well, you can enjoy a break from parenting. It will enhance your vacation and refresh you.

TAKE A BREAK CHECK LIST

Our Notes:

- *Explore child care alternatives before traveling*
- *Travel with another family*
- *Take a trusted sitter with you*
  Write up a contract
- *Employ a child care service*
  Ask about qualifications
- *Use day-care at resorts*
  Gather information before leaving home
- *Ask relatives for help*
- *Explain rules and leave emergency numbers with anyone*
  caring for your child

Your Notes:

TAKE YOUR CHILDREN AND GO

Traveling with more than one child can be adventurous or chaotic--it's all in the planning. Travel agents who specialize in family travel can be your key to salvation. These agents are informed about tours, rates and destinations that appeal to families. If your area does not have an agency that specializes in family travel, look for an agent who has children or has an interest in this area.

A good agent will watch for specials, keep you informed about what is available, and will know the best times to travel to your destination. Your agent should know about day care, kids rates, facilities and points of interest. She can work with you to arrange for the best routes and seats for flying. When working with an agent, be clear about your needs and desires. Report back to her on how your travel and facilities measured up.

Let children who are old enough participate in the planning. Talk about the options that are available. Give everyone an opportunity to say what he wants to do during the vacation. Include your desires in this planning too. Mom may want to spend time visiting her sister, Robin may want to go to the zoo, Shelley wants to ride the subway, Dad wants to take in a play, and baby Annie needs a nap every afternoon. Arranging the schedule and compromising before you leave home helps make the trip one the whole family can enjoy.

Packing

An emergency bag should be packed which holds many of the solutions to travel problems. A parent should consider carrying:

•Gum, orange slices, or something for everyone to chew on when changing altitude. Even older children have trouble clearing their ears while flying or when driving through the mountains.

•A book that appeals to a variety of ages for reading aloud. Consult your public librarian or the appendix for suggestions. Think about reading "the next exciting chapter" while you are waiting at the airport, those last 50 miles of the day or while waiting for your meal in the restaurant.

•Individual pages of mazes, puzzles, or dot-to-dot activities.

They fit into a pocket or purse and can be pulled out when needed.

•Pencils or crayons for decorating the back of place mats while waiting for dinner.

•A deck of cards. Children too young to play conventional card games can make up matching or counting games, lay out the cards, make "roads" or build card "houses".

•A supply of colored dot stickers and/or picture stickers and paper. This combination can keep preschoolers occupied for an amazing length of time.

•Cellophane tape and plain paper can be used to create an "art gallery", block the sun in the car window or fashion an airplane. Look for some specially designed tape like "Hello Kitty" or Sesame Street to make it extra special.

•Small surprises, maybe even wrapped, to be brought out when time on the trip hangs heavy. For example, when visiting with relatives who have no children or no toys, a tiny box of Legos, a new miniature car or a new coloring book may provide the diversion to keep your child entertained while you enjoy your visit. Since these surprises are "buy time" insurance, avoid anything that requires boisterous play, needs adult supervision or makes a mess!

•Food. Always have something handy--fruit, trail mix, crackers, etc.

•First aid kit with bandages, Tylenol, wet wipes, etc.

Each child should have a backpack or small bag marked with their name and address. This bag should carry your child's essentials such as his special blanket or teddy bear, a couple of books that are familiar and can be looked at or "read" on his own, one or two favorite toys, and a small flashlight to reduce anxiety of sleeping away from home.

Take a minute at each transition point to have each child check his bag for all those important belongings. He should check the floor, under seats or chairs and in the seat pockets for toys, books and teddy. Your child should be responsible for his own treasures.

Each child should have identification stating name, home address, phone, destination and any important medical information such as allergies or conditions. An ID bracelet would supply most of this information. If your child does not have one, write this information out and put it in your child's shoe. (See Appendix for source to order identification tags and bracelets.)

Options

While traveling, children should participate in the world and excitement around them, but parents and kids sometimes need "getaway" time. A small walkman type cassette player, with ear phones can provide everyone with a break. A set of stories that a parent has taped ahead of time, the latest rock music, a collection of children's songs or even some old Bill Cosby stories can give adults time to talk or take a snooze.

When traveling by car, frequent bathroom breaks can be a problem. Consider taking a squirt bottle of water along . The novelty of the spray combined with the limited amount of water actually consumed, helps kids take in less fluids, thus extending the times between "pit stops".

Kids will be Kids

The breathtaking view of the Grand Canyon may fill you with awe, but your kids may be too busy fighting over a stick of gum to notice. **Be realistic about your expectations of your kids**. They need variety, room to move, frequent feeding and reassurance in new situations. Parents usually understand this when their children are babies or toddlers, but often forget this when kids are school age. Be flexible. Don't try to enforce all the same rules that you use at home--that's what vacations are all about--for children and adults.

Not all traveling is designed with kids in mind. A class reunion, wedding or funeral may cause your children to hang on your legs because of the stress of unfamiliar surroundings and people. If there are other children present, they may not warm up to each other until five minutes before it is time to leave.

If the event takes place where there is room to play outside, stop at a drug/discount store for some provisions--a ball, jump rope, jacks or bubbles. If the function is indoors, try a

cardboard puzzle, drawing supplies or a new book. Find space for your children to play or explore. Rotate adults supervising. Don't expect your kids to be able to handle these situations for an extended time without some breaks or diversions. Being on best behavior among adult strangers is taxing and stressful.

Develop a ritual or traditions that can be repeated on every family trip or vacation. Rituals provide a necessary and comforting familiar element for children when faced with the anxiety of the unknown. They are also the basis for lifelong memories. Your custom might be as simple as a particular food that you rarely eat at home, but ALWAYS eat on vacation, such as individual boxes of sugary cereal for breakfast. It could be those special songs that you ALWAYS sing together while driving. Or, your ritual may be as complicated as composing a family diary or home movie of your adventures.

I Wanna Sit By the Window

Every parent who has taken kids in the car for more than a twenty minute ride, knows the value of seat rotation and strategic seating as a way to limit bickering. The same works for air travel. Whether your seats are in a row, separated by the aisle or in different parts of the plane, where your children sit can affect the quality of your trip. Parents sitting across the aisle from each other can provide walking space for a toddler. Having seats in different parts of the plane can give you some options such as relief for or from strangers sitting around you, a change of scenery, increased possibility of sitting near other kids, a change to a quieter or darker part of the plane, a chance for more room, or a seat with a view of the movie.

TAKE YOUR CHILDREN AND GO CHECK LIST

Our Notes:

- *Let the kids participate in the planning*
- *Pack an "emergency" bag with provisions to keep kids occupied*
- *Be realistic about your expectations; give kids a break from rules*
- *Develop a ritual for all family vacations*
- *Utilize seat rotation and strategic seating*

Your Notes:

WHEN YOUR CHILD HAS HEALTH CONCERNS

Traveling with a child who has a chronic medical condition presents a great challenge, even to experienced parents. If the condition is controlled, only small modifications may be needed, and your travel will be as pleasurable as that of other families'. If the condition is subject to frequent or threatening flare ups, you may find the thought of travel and coping with the additional unknowns unappealing. If this is the case, read on. Planning and practice can make travel another conquerable obstacle in dealing with your child's special needs.

Start With Short Trips

Don't give up traveling. Short day trips or overnight trips can refresh and help family members maintain a balance between caretaking and fun--something important for parents of children with special needs. These trips can be undertaken on short notice, require less commitment in terms of time and money, and offer the security of being near your normal medical facilities and home should a problem arise.

When searching for last minute accommodations, an automobile association lodging guide can be invaluable. These books provide up-to-date listings of motels and hotels along with phone numbers, costs, available facilities and local points of interest. Camping guidebooks contain names of hospitals nearest camp areas.

Do your own research. Keep notes on places you would like to visit. Talk to friends and other families about their travels. If an area is booked up, ask if all reservations are confirmed;

if not, there may be a chance of cancellation and you can ask to be put on a waiting list. In any case, always find out if there are "off" times when business is slower and your chances are better at getting last minute accommodations.

Preparation is important for short trips. If your child needs medication on a regular schedule, ask your pharmacist to prepare some of the prescriptions in smaller containers.

 Place essential medications in the glove compartment of the vehicles you commonly use in case you forget your normal supply. If you use more than one car, label each prescription with the car name so if it is removed it is apparent which car is missing its supply. It is important to remember that a glove compartment temperature can be 50 degrees hotter than the inside of your car. If your child's medications are temperature sensitive, move the medication to a cooler place when traveling in hot weather.

Zip lock bags are handy traveling items. They can hold medicines together in a packet. A small card in the packet explaining when and how to administer medications helps when leaving your child with grandparents or sitters.

Zip lock bags can also be filled with crushed ice to make cold packs for reducing swelling or used as a car sickness bag.

Long Trips

Even with serious health problems there will be times and occasions when the extra risks and hassles of a long trip will be outweighed by the opportunity to get a distant change of scenery, be part of an historic family reunion, or take advantage of a business trip to an exciting foreign country.

Start by thinking through and researching the situations you may encounter in your travels. Evaluate these situations in terms of what your child can tolerate, then seek out the options that best meet your family's needs.

For instance, if you are taking your seriously asthmatic child on a visit to your brother's household which you know includes two indoor cats, you could start by asking your brother to farm out the cats one week prior to your visit. Offer to pay half the cost of having the carpets cleaned before you arrive. If this is not reasonable for him, you may want to consider staying in a pet-free motel nearby. If this is too expensive, ask your brother about arranging for you to stay with non-smoking friends or relatives in the area that don't have pets.

Local support groups of parents whose children have similar conditions can be a great source of information for planning your travels.

Well in advance of your departure, check with your pediatrician and specialist. Discuss how to go about calling them long distance if you or an out of area physician needs to consult with them about your child's medical condition and treatment.

For emergencies, your doctor may be able to recommend a specific doctor or clinic in the area that you will be staying. If warranted, ask your doctor to write out a summary of your child's medical condition, the current treatment and specific recommendations for emergencies. This will be of great help to another physician caring for your child.

If you are in a strange city and need medical care for your child, you can look in the yellow or white pages under "Physician's Information and Referral Services." These services may be operated by the county medical association or private hospitals. They will give you the name of local participating physicians. The amount of screening used in selecting physicians varies by area and agency. You will want to ask specifics as to areas of specialty and age groups treated when you call.

Another way of locating a reputable physician is to check with a good quality hotel in the area. Usually they can give you the name of physicians they recommend for their hotel guests.

If you are going to an out of the way vacation spot and your child can only take a certain type of medication such as an antibiotic, ask your doctor for an appropriate supply to take with you. Often small clinics and pharmacies in vacation areas stock only commonly used drugs and may not have your special medication available for a day or more. If traveling to foreign countries, ask for a complete supply to take with you. Use only under a doctor's supervision.

Always bring the basics: decongestant, Tylenol, thermometer and any other special items that are essential for your child. Carry essential medications with you in your purse, carry-on luggage or diaper bag because suitcases can easily become lost or misplaced leading to major problems if all your child's medication is in them.

When planning your trip, always plan for the emergency quick trip home. Find out which carriers honor each other's

tickets. While at an airport, ask for printed flight schedules from all the airline carriers you might use. Having this information will give you time frames for making a quick decision to return home. This is extremely helpful in a foreign country where using the phone system and getting clear and correct information in a foreign language can seem like an insurmountable obstacle when hurried and stressed.

If you are traveling to a foreign country, look for a medical travel advisory book at your local library or public health department. Find out as much as you can about the conditions and precautions regarding the area such as recent outbreaks of illness and needed immunizations and medications.

You may want to locate an English speaking native from the country you plan to visit. Have them write a note in the language and script of the country explaining the special needs you child may have. For instance, if you are going to Japan and your child is allergic to certain foods your note written in Kanji might read:

> *My daughter is very allergic to eggs, nuts and milk. Please show me the items on the menu that do not contain any of these ingredients. If you are not sure, would you please ask the cook?   Thank you.*

Each time you eat out, simply hand the note to your waiter when ordering. If necessary, he can take it to the cook and you will be assured the message will not be lost in translation between your table and the kitchen. This can be indispensable in taking the guesswork out of ordering food for children with special dietary needs.

Similar notes can also be helpful in communicating with pharmacies or physicians regarding your child's prescriptions, drug allergies or any other special medical conditions or requirements.

If you do not know any foreign speaker personally, check with the foreign language departments of local colleges or language schools. Take time in working with your translator to make sure he understands your message. Have him repeat it back to you. You may want to have these notes laminated so they stand up to repeated use.

Whether traveling locally or abroad, it is easy to get carried away in trying to see and do as much as possible. For some children, being hurried and in unfamiliar surroundings can make them more vulnerable to illness. Try to incorporate small segments of your everyday routine in your daily vacation schedule. Simple things such as story time before bed, or your normal afternoon walk can help children maintain a sense of home. Aim for a slower pace, making sure both you and your child get adequate rest and quiet time. Keeping stress at bay is an important part of staying healthy for all of us.

WHEN YOUR CHILD HAS HEALTH CONCERNS CHECK LIST

Our Notes:

•Think through situations and options
•Check with pediatrician before leaving
•Discuss contacting your physician after hours
•Always bring basics
•Bring any special medications that may be needed
•Check medical travel advisory for any foreign areas you
 plan to visit
•Allow for plenty of rest and quiet time
•Get special notes written in native language

Your Notes:

CONCLUSION

As new parents you have learned to see the world through a different eye. You can look around a room and see all the dangers that will attract your little one. Your hearing is acute. You know what little sounds to ignore or rush to.

As traveling parents you will also develop new skills. This book is just a start. Some of the ideas you may embrace, others you may reject. Hopefully you will find some ideas that work for you and your baby.

Be sure to give everything you have a second look. It may not work in your home, but it may be perfect for travel.

There are many costly products that can take away from your traveling budget. Some may be worth it because it is just what you need, others can be improvised with things you have around the house.

There is also a world out there ready to serve you and your traveling needs. You are a consumer. They want your money and they want you to be pleased. Let them know when they do it right and let them know when high chairs are broken or areas are unsafe.

If you find yourself saving samples, looking at off-peak rates at resorts or dusting off your old suitcase, then it may be getting closer to the time when you should take your baby and go!

APPENDIX

The following resources may help you in various aspects of your travels:

Consumer Reports Books Guide to Baby Products
by Sandy Jones with Werner Freitag and the Editors of Consumer Reports Books
Consumers Union, Mt.Vernon, NY, 1988

An excellent evaluation of brand name baby products and equipment as well as advice on how to choose the best products for your needs.

Traveling Games for Babies
A Handbook of Games for Infants to Five-Year Olds by Julie Hagstrom
A & W Visual Library, New York, 1981

A collection of ingenious game ideas to keep children amused throughout vacation travel. Especially helpful are the quiet games to calm an active toddler.

W.A. Morrow Co, Inc
P.O. Box 80
Mercer Island, WA 98040
(206)392-8908

Company that specializes in I.D. bracelets, tags, necklaces, etc. for children. They provide fast reliable service and have been in business since 1950.

Story books that are appropriate for a wide range of ages:

Atwater	Mr. Popper's Penguins
Cleary	Ramona
"	Ramona the Pest
Dahl	B.F.G.
Field	Hitty-Her First 100 Years
Grahame	Wind in the Willows
Lowry	All About Sam
Milne	Winnie the Pooh
White	Charlotte's Web
Wilder	Little House in the Big Woods

For more suggestions check **The Read Aloud Handbook** or **The New Read Aloud Handbook**, by Jim Trelease. These give some excellent suggestions for books appropriate for many ages.

Consider also the wide selection of books on tape that are available at your local bookstore or public library. This is especially helpful for those parents who get carsick looking at anything more than a quick peek at the map!

Portable High Chair

This portable high chair stows compactly in your diaper bag for use in restaurants, at the homes of friends and relatives, or any situation in which a high chair is unavailable. At home, a TV tray or low table pulled up to the chair will provide a tray area for feeding utensils.

Construction Time: Approximately 15 minutes

1. Use a piece of cloth about 20 X 53 inches (standard pillowcase with seams removed). Cut two 7 1/2 X 20 inch strips from one end and set aside. Turn and zigzag all edges on remaining piece.

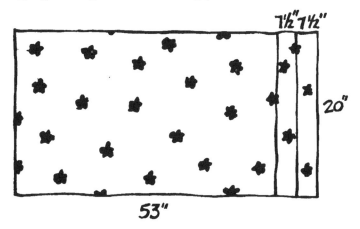

2. Fold eight inches from top and stitch at sides.

(Portable High Chair is continued on the next two pages.)

(Portable High Chair Continued)

3. Turn bottom corners to center front and sew along
   each edge.

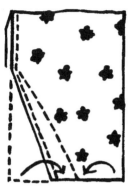

4. Fold cloth strips in half, sew 1/4" seams on three
   sides, turn and press to make straps.

5. Attach straps with zigzag or by using 1/8" seam.

(Please see next page for final instructions.)

(Portable High Chair Continued)

6. To Use: Place folded corners over back of chair, spreading cloth down over the seat. Place baby on chair, bringing straps between legs, to baby's stomach and tie behind chair.

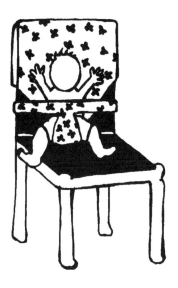

73

INDEX

NOTES:

Also Available from Bear Creek Publications:

No Bored Babies

Here is the indispensible guide that takes you step by step through babies' developmental stages from birth to age two, with ideas for making toys appropriate to each new skill level. Contains over 100 toy ideas and more than 75 illustrations.

$4.95•64 Pages•Perfect Bound

To receive your copy of *No Bored Babies*, complete the order form on the next page.

You may order additional copies of **TAKE YOUR BABY AND GO!** direct from the publisher. It makes a great gift for friends, new or expectant parents.

Please send me:
____ copies of TAKE YOUR BABY AND GO! at $5.95 ea.
____ copies of NO BORED BABIES at $4.95 ea.

Name _____

Address _____

City _____ State _____ Zip _____

Sales Tax: Please add 8.1% for books shipped to Washington addresses.

Shipping: Add $1.00 for first book and 50 cents for each additional book.

Payment:
_____ Check
_____ Credit Card ____ Visa ____ MasterCard
Card Number: _____
Name on Card: _____
Exp. date: _____/_____

Send payment to:
BEAR CREEK PUBLICATIONS
2507 Minor Avenue East
Seattle, WA 98102
(206) 322-7604

Telephone Orders: Call *Toll Free* 1-800-326-6566. Have your Visa or MasterCard ready.

Discounts available for larger orders. Call or write for details.